Grandma's Smile

Story by Pamela Rushby

Illustrations by Chantal Stewart

Rigby PM Plus Chapter Books
part of the Rigby PM Program
Emerald Level

U.S. edition © 2003 Rigby Education
A division of Reed Elsevier Inc.
1000 Hart Road
Barrington, IL 60010 - 2627
www.rigby.com

Text © 2003 Pamela Rushby
Illustrations © 2003 Thomson Learning Australia
Originally published in Australia by Thomson Learning Australia

10 9 8 7 6 5 4 3 2 1
07 06 05 04 03

Grandma's Smile
    ISBN 0 7578 4114 7

Printed in China by Midas Printing (Asia) Ltd

Contents

Chapter 1
Sunday

Last week, my grandpa died.

Today, Grandma came from the country. She is going to stay with us for a few weeks.

"Grandma's feeling very unhappy right now," Mom said to me. "She needs us to look after her for a while."

We are all feeling very unhappy about Grandpa. We know that Grandma is sad too, and we want to help her. But our house is very small. We live in an apartment behind our bakery, near the middle of the city.

I said to Mom and Dad, "I could sleep on a mattress on the floor in your room, and Grandma could have my room."

"That's nice of you, Trudy," said Mom and Dad. So that's what we did.

When Grandma came, she hugged me, like she always does. But she didn't smile when she saw me, like she always does. She looked sad.

When she saw the room we'd prepared for her, she looked even sadder. She said, "I didn't want to put you out of your room, Trudy. I could have slept on the couch in the living room."

I told her it was okay.

I hoped she'd feel happier now. I hoped she'd smile.

But she didn't.

Chapter 2

Monday

When I got home from school today, Mom and Dad were working in the bakery, like they always do.

"Where's Grandma?" I asked.

"She's sitting on the couch," said Mom. She looked worried. "She's been there all day. I can't get her to go out."

Mom looked at me.

"Trudy, we're very busy. I can't leave the store. Could you take Grandma out for a little walk?"

"Sure," I said.

Mom smiled at me. "Thanks, dear," she said. "Try to make her smile."

9

I went to get Grandma. "Try to make her smile," Mom had said. What sort of thing would make Grandma smile, I wondered. I didn't know.

Then I had an idea. What if I showed Grandma some of the things that make me smile?

I thought about it. There are lots of things in our suburb that make me smile. It was worth a try.

So I took Grandma for a walk past Mr. Windsor's house.

Mr. Windsor lives in a tiny old house down a side street. He has a very small garden in front. But his garden is absolutely packed full of roses. Most of the roses are a pale pink like kittens' noses. But some are a bright pink, and some are as white as snow. They lean over the fence and climb up the walls of the house. They smell wonderful. Some days, hot still summer days, you can smell them right around the corner, before you see them.

I showed Grandma Mr. Windsor's roses. "How beautiful, Trudy!" she said.

Mr. Windsor came out to the garden.

"Hello, Mr. Windsor," I said. "This is my grandma."

"Pleased to meet you," Mr. Windsor said.

Mr. Windsor took a pair of scissors out of his pocket and cut one of the most beautiful roses. It was a lovely soft pink, with frills at the edges of the petals. He gave it to Grandma.

Grandma thanked him very politely. She took a deep breath of the rose's scent.

I watched her hopefully.

But she didn't smile.

Chapter 3

Tuesday

This afternoon Grandma and I walked over to Nuyens' fruit store and walked around to the back of the store.

"We buy all of our fruit from Nuyens," I told Grandma. "Their cat has just had kittens. Mrs. Nuyen said that I can have one of them."

"That's nice, Trudy," said Grandma.

I took Grandma to the shed at the back of the fruit store. "Look!" I said, as I opened the door. "The kittens are in here."

In a cardboard box in the shed lay the Nuyens' cat and four kittens – two ginger, one black, and one black and white. The cat purred when she saw me.

I knelt down to stroke the kittens gently.

Mrs. Nuyen came into the shed. "Trudy's going to take one of the kittens when they're old enough," she told Grandma. "They're big enough for you to hold now, Trudy. Let us know when you decide which one you want."

I picked up the black kitten and gave it to Grandma to hold. She cuddled the tiny kitten up to her warm sweater. It purred and snuggled into her chin. "Oh, what a darling kitten!" she said.

I watched her hopefully.

But she didn't smile.

Chapter 4
Wednesday

Today I took Grandma to the Albertis' ice cream store. It's my favorite store in the whole street. The Albertis make more ice cream flavors than you could imagine. They call them gelati.

The gelati are stored in deep containers behind a glass counter. They're all colors – pale pink and deep orange and soft green and darkest chocolate brown.

Some of the flavors are creamy, and some are sharp and cool. Mom had given me some money so that Grandma and I could each have an ice-cream cone.

Vanilla Strawberry Chocolate

berry Lemon-lime Orange 21

I never know which flavor to choose. Sometimes, Mr. Alberti gives me a little taste of different flavors so that I can make up my mind.

Today, he told me that he had a new flavor – lemon-lime sherbet. He gave Grandma and me our ice-cream cones.

"What do you think?" he said.

The lemon-lime was sharp and cool, and the sherbet sparkled on our tongues.

"Yummy!" I said.

"Absolutely delicious," said Grandma.

I watched her hopefully.

But she didn't smile.

Chapter 5

Thursday

Today I took Grandma to the library. Thursday afternoon is story day at the library. The kids all sit on the floor, and Mr. Lawson, the librarian, reads us stories. Grandma didn't have to sit on the floor. Mr. Lawson found her a chair.

Today it was a story about balloons, and at the end there was a special surprise. Mr. Lawson had a balloon for each of us! The balloons were filled with helium that made them float.

Mr. Lawson gave me a blue balloon, and he gave Grandma a red one.

We walked home with our balloons bobbing above our heads. They had very long strings, so we could let them go up and up, and then pull them back down again.

Grandma let her balloon go up and up, red against the blue and white sky, and then pulled it down again.

I watched her hopefully.

But she didn't smile.

Chapter 6

Friday

Today I took Grandma to the Kumars' grocery store. It's not an ordinary grocery store. The Kumars sell lots of special things for Asian cooking.

Their store has a rich, heavy, spicy smell. There's cinnamon in it, and cloves, and pepper, and lots of other things all mixed up, which make the smell.

At the back of the store, the Kumars' baby was asleep in his crib. We peeped in at him. He wriggled and yawned and opened his eyes and made a little squeaky noise.

Mrs. Kumar came over. She picked the baby up, and smiled at Grandma. Mrs. Kumar doesn't speak much English, but she held the baby out, offering him to Grandma to hold.

Grandma took the baby and held him gently. She stroked his fluffy little head. He burped loudly.

I watched Grandma hopefully.

But she didn't smile.

Chapter 7

Saturday

Today I had time to take Grandma for a longer walk. We went to the park. It's about six blocks away. There's a pond in the park, with ducks, and lots of flowers, and a kids' playground with swings.

Mom had given us a bag of stale bread to feed the ducks. We threw pieces of bread to the ducks, and watched them quack and splash and dive and chase each other, fighting for the bread.

Some of the ducks were brown, and when they flapped their wings they had shiny deep green and blue feathers under them. Water flew from their wings, like sparkling diamonds in the sun. Some of it splashed on us.

I watched Grandma hopefully.

But she didn't smile.

29

When the bread was gone, Grandma said, "Would you like to play on the swings for a while, Trudy?" So we went over to the playground.

There was someone at the swings I knew. It was Eleni, from my class at school. She was sitting on a bench with a very small old lady all dressed in black. The old lady had her head down, looking at her feet. She wasn't smiling.

"That's my yiayia," said Eleni. "She's just come from Greece. She's going to live with us now. She's sad because my papou died."

Grandma looked at the old lady. She sat down close to her on the bench. The old lady raised her head and looked up at Grandma.

"Hello," said Grandma.

"My yiayia doesn't speak English," Eleni said.

Grandma looked at the old lady again. She reached out and took her hand. She held it between both of hers, and patted it gently.

And Grandma smiled.